C.S. Hart

On Enemy Lines

Reviews

On Enemy Lines. The reality and truth of spiritual warfare is fascinating to some, fearful to others, and maybe not even thought about by many. This read is helpful and encouraging and brings an understanding as well as hope and victory! C.S. Hart has great understanding to help bring those searching to come out on the winning end of becoming a conqueror and an overcomer!

Gene J. Hall, Pastor of Warrenton Community Church. Warrenton, Missouri.

***

Windstone:The Secrets Within deals with the unrealized spiritual problems we face in today's society. Spiritual warfare is real, but people have trouble believing in what they can't always see. This story is like an onion; you peel away the layers, and try to figure out the twists with the character Willa. She shares a candid look of a woman fighting the principalities tearing at our lives every day. Even though it's considered fiction, it strikes a powerfully true chord. A great illustration of how darkness can't hide in the light!

Mitch Hall, Media Ministries, Bridge of Hope Church, Paris, TN

Windstone: The Secrets Within held many secrets. This suspense novel had my mind racing throughout the entire story. I feared for Willa, and then wondered if the demons she fought were real or in her mind. Each chapter kept me guessing and wanting questions answered. I enjoyed C.S. Hart's first novel and look forward to many more.

J. Hatcher, Arkansas Educator, Corning, Arkansas.

ON ENEMY LINES Copyright © 2014 by C.S. Hart

Published by Media Land Publishing.   Library of Congress Cataloging.

Unless otherwise indicated, all scriptures quotations are taken from the Holy Bible, "New International Version". NIV copyright © 1973, 1978, 1984 by the International Bible Society.   Used by permission of Zondervan, All Rights Reserved.

Quantity sales: Special discounts are available on quantity purchases by corporations, associations, churches and others. For details, contact HartStrings Studios, 406 East Walton, Warrenton, Missouri, 63383.

Orders by U.S. trade bookstores and wholesalers. Please contact Barnes and Noble at barnesandnoble.com

ISBN-10: 061595264X

ISBN-13: 9780615952642

1.   Christian Living.   2.   Spiritual Warfare.   3. Facing the Enemy.

Printed in the United States of America

On Enemy Lines

By C.S. Hart

Acknowledgments

Special thanks to:

- My husband, Dale, for praying for me and encouraging me when I felt like this project would never end. You are my biggest fan...I love you!

- My children, Brittany, Christian and Son-in – law Andrew, for being patient during my crazy schedule and daily demands.

- My church family of Warrenton Community Church, for believing in me and cheering me on through each endeavor.

- And, above all, my eternal thanks goes to the Lord Jesus Christ, who "Sacrificed All" so I could dwell with Him forever. I will daily, moment by moment follow YOU!

CONTENTS

FORWARD

Forward

"The Lord causes my enemies who rise up against me to be defeated before my face; they shall come out against me one way and flee before me seven ways." Deuteronomy 28:7

The salvation of Christ is a beautiful and very intimate covenant between you and your Savior. When you choose to give your heart to God and accept the gift offered to you by the sacrifice Jesus gave freely on the cross, you enter into a life of forgiveness, mercy and grace. After all, it's more than the promise of eternal life that wins most souls over to the Kingdom...it's the realization of having a relationship with a loving Father, a trustworthy Savior and a comforting Spirit that is ever-present in this life of distress turmoil and heartbreak.

As an evangelistic couple who has served God through all the trials this life can dish out, my husband and I have seen the delusion that many buy into when they surrender to God.

First, allow me to say that God is absolute love, unfailing strength, and an ever-present help in times of need.   However, to think that salvation means a quick ticket out of trouble is a deception in itself.   What we must understand in this world of corrupt sin is that God gives us the tools and wisdom to battle the darkest of foes.

When the Word says the enemy goes about seeking whom he may devour, it is said as a WARNING!...to the righteous...the ones who daily try to live upright and holy.   The enemy is very conscious of those going about practicing evil or deliberately fleeing from Godliness.   He does not seek these people...for they are not a threat to him.   No, he seeks out...persistently searches, and deliberately chooses to torment the children of his opposition...GOD!

Don't let this make you discouraged and please don't lose heart. There is GREAT news for all who serve the Almighty God.

Romans 8:37 *says this, "I am more than a conqueror through Christ who loves me."*

This scripture should give you cause to gird up....stand strong...and face the enemy through every attack that may come.

GOOD NEWS!!!

It should make you feel special and chosen when trials come against you.

No, I didn't say you would feel good....I said the good news is you should feel honored that Satan views you as a threat. After all, the Bible tells us to rejoice in our sufferings.

Why does God allow us to suffer?

Through my experience I can honestly tell you, it is for your own benefit. Some of the most horrible times in my life have molded and shaped me into a more dedicated and determined follower of Jesus Christ. Isn't that what we are striving for anyway?

As you read this book, you will begin to sense a desire...a stirring...an unquenched fire in these passages. I pray you will feel, through these pages, how passionate I am about my Father; how grateful I am to my Savior; and how very in love I am with the Holy Spirit!

C.S.Hart

*O*n Enemy Lines

A Guide to Spiritual Warfare

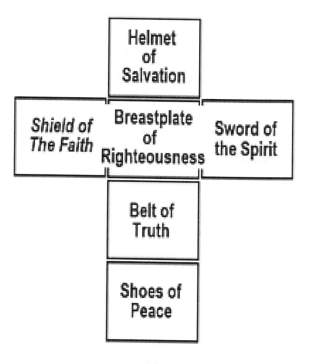

Chapter

1

CONFIDENCE

"I am determined and confident! I am not afraid or discouraged, for the Lord my God is with me wherever I go." **Joshua 1:19**

When I was a child I realized very quickly that the people who succeeded were the people who stood confident in themselves. I struggled with this. You see, I had a number of obstacles in my home which created in me a *not so confident* child. However, after living a life full of struggles I have concluded that God was always very prevalent in my surroundings. Having come through so many trials, I have seen that I must be determined to become confident in who I am—

----a child of the living God!

With that in mind, I want you to realize that you too must live a confident life.

Confident in who you are...in knowing why you are here...and realizing what you can do to enlarge the Kingdom of God.

After you become confident in the security of who you are, why you are here and what you can do—then you will be a mighty force to be reckoned with. The enemy will not be able to withstand all you dish out.

You see, Satan preys on your fear, insecurities and failures. When you become confident, he no longer has a leg to stand on— and...

*Your fear of failure is gone...

*Your fear of acceptance is gone...

*Your fear of unworthiness is gone...

*Your fear of being useless is gone...

When you realize you are a **SUCCESS**—you are **WORTHY** and you are **USEFUL** to God's Kindgom, the enemy has to flee because you are walking in the truth of who God is...then when the spiritual warfare begins...(and it will), you will be equipped with the weapons to **WIN!**

Psalm 18:29 says, *"With your help I can advance against a troop; with my God I can scale a wall."*

This sounds like it was written by someone pretty confident...pretty secure in his ability through the help of his comrade.

When you allow God to lead your life and put yourself in His hands, it takes the pressure off of your abilities. We all know that our human strengths and abilities are not enough to prevail in this world of such evil and unrighteousness. We all must become SUPERNATURAL!!!

David understood this when he stood in front of Goliath. He did not rely on his size, muscle strength or agility. He knew to let go and let God. By taking himself out of the equation he realized God could use him (no matter his stature or physical strength) to overcome even the largest of obstacles.

Whatever that obstacle may be, know that God can and will help you up and over it. He will guide you around it, and He will bring you through it.

HE WILL DELIVER YOU.

Just remain steadfast in your faith. Your confidence will begin to skyrocket with each test you pass, each trial you face and each temptation you overcome. God wants you to know who you are...HIS! He wants you to stand strong and dodge those fiery darts of the enemy with grace and dignity and if it need be...**Holy Boldness** and **Righteous**

Anger... You say that you believe in Him?   Well, what you need to let saturate into your soul is that **HE** believes in you. He gave you the power so He knows you can do it. It is hard...it is a battle...He never said it would be easy, but He does say He is an ever-present help in times of trouble. I don't know about you, but that sounds good to me. It gives me the hope and understanding that I can do all things, face all things, and overcome all things through Christ Who strengthens me. AMEN!!!

THINK ON THIS

Who are you?

Why are you here?

Where are you going?

NOTES

CHAPTER

2

DO WHAT?

What exactly is being on enemy lines? *It is spiritual warfare...the most important thing you must do as a Christian.* **Your life depends on it.**

In **Ephesians 6:12**, Paul writes:

"For our struggle is not against flesh and blood, but against the rulers, against the authorities, against the

powers of this dark world and against the spiritual forces of evil in the heavenly realms."

It's not about our neighbor, co-worker or spouse who is fighting against us, the ones who cut you to the bone with insults or negative comments. It's not primarily against the person who's opposing us, who just hurt us, who is blocking our way at work—it is instead against what Paul calls the rulers, the authorities, the powers of this dark world and the spiritual forces of evil in the heavenly realms.

The bad news....

- If you are a Christian you have a real ENEMY!

The good news...

- If you are a Christian you are equipped to fight and WIN!

This enemy is unseen...on the down low...hiding under the beds of our lives, in the dark closets of our pasts, in the cobwebs of our secrets, this enemy is evil.

He's invisible, he's evil and he's on the attack.

Oh no....!!! What do we do?

Do we immediately go to the word of God on a daily basis? When the routine of life bears down on us, do we say, "So God, show me what to do"? Or do we tend to make our own choices and decisions? Does the will of God take precedence in our regular day to day schedule? It should...but does it?

Most always we get caught up in our own abilities and make our own decisions...our own way seems to take first place on our totem pole called life.

When things get bad...*and they do sometimes*, we should run to Him and lay it all on His shoulders....this is what He asked us to do, isn't it? Of course.   But do we? No, not ordinarily. We look at the circumstances and all of a sudden become overwhelmed with the "what are we gonna do's", and "how am I gonna get through this one?"   And when we get caught up in what "*we*" are going to do, we lose sight of what "***HE***" is going to do. After all, He is the source of positivity...the glue that holds us together...the very breath and blood that runs through our veins.

In order to achieve victory over our circumstances and overcome all obstacles of opposition we must strive to be like Christ.

Romans 13:14 says,   "But put ye on the Lord Jesus Christ, and make not provision for the flesh, to fulfill the lusts thereof."

Can we do that?

Of course we can.

But how do we accomplish this when the whole world is falling down around us? When the storms of life are raging so viciously that we can't see a foot in front of our face? When the clouds of doubt and confusion are blowing so heavily, weighing us down with pain and grief? How can we walk in the path that He walked? Putting on the righteousness of His glory? The answer is ....

...one step at a time.

With each moment of each day, we must choose very consciously to walk in His ways. To make decisions clearly and decisively. To listen and hear HIS answer for our lives.

What happens if we don't...?

The enemy comes in and pounces. Up and down...driving our strength into the ground until we have none left.

You need to remember one thing and never forget it.......

The enemy is out there waiting...just waiting to take you out.

When you focus on living for God and doing His will instead of your own, you find yourself convicted each time a wrong thought enters your mind.   Conviction....(ahhh don't be scared of this word) It's actually a good thing.

If you feel convicted it means your spirit acknowledges wrong-doing. It means you care about what you do...what choices you make...the places you go, and the things you choose to have in your home. Do you know how many people don't think twice about these things? They say, "Oh, lighten up...live a little." Well, I personally choose to live the righteous way. The way God would want for me. I want to make Him proud, don't you?

Satan will put so many things in your path. Temptations to slow you down or to turn you in a different direction. He will do anything he can to make you think the world has more to offer. The media is a BIG one. Television, movies, games, any kind of entertainment is the things he can use to his benefit. Don't get me wrong, there is nothing wrong with family time and having movie or t.v and game time...nothing at all. But beware...we must edit our homes. We must rate the programs we watch even as adults. I thoroughly believe that if someone under the age of 17 shouldn't watch a movie then I, as a Christian, should not entertain myself with it either. Remember, you are the editor of your home....take this job seriously; it can dictate the atmosphere you live in. Satan would love nothing more than to invade and destroy.

Put your barriers up...bring up the drawbridge and protect your fortress. It is your job and it is a big part of Spiritual warfare.

Satan wants to kill you. He wants to damage you so greatly that you feel used and abused and get angry with God. He wants you so angry with God that you curse him and die, just as Job's wife told him to do. But just like Job, we must stay focused on the truth of who God is and not the circumstances that fall upon you....after all, it rains on the just as well as the unjust...correct?

THINK ON THIS...

How does conviction help us in our spiritual walk?

How do you guard your fortress (your home)? What is important to you to keep out of your daily life?

How does this make us closer to God?

NOTES

Chapter

3

RECOGNIZING THE ENEMY

If you are going through an emotional trial; something you seem to just not be able to face, how do you know if it is an attack of the enemy or a trial by God?

This very question is a tough one for some people. God uses things in our lives to bring us to a higher level spiritually; however, Satan also attacks us to bring us further away from God. Distinguishing between the two can cause some people such confusion they give up the fight altogether.

The one thing we have to remember is that God is never NOT there.

He is always there in the midst of everything. It is **our choice** that causes the outcome. Did you get that?   It is our choice...our responses...our actions that cause the outcome.

Here is a story about an incident that happened to me during my course of teaching high school...

I worked for a Christian school and was graciously, not only allowed to speak of my faith, but encouraged to do so each day.   I had a student who we will call Billy. Billy came in on his first day and proclaimed immediately that he did not want to hear of this *so called* Jesus. He had a predetermined idea of who God was and nothing was going to change his mind.   Every day he would come into my English classroom with one thing in mind...to denounce the God that his teacher served. He was adamant about stating his opinion on atheism. This was disturbing to me. I prayed for Billy silently during school and outwardly in my private time. The other teachers had similar problems with him. I never failed to give God the Glory during each day and even prayed during class, which we were so honored to be able to do. Billy grew more and more agitated each day. I knew holding back on my beliefs would be detrimental to his future. This young man needed to see grounded believers standing strong, not someone who would back down in the face of the enemy.

Before I go on I want to share with you what the Apostle Paul said long ago....

Paul writes in 2 Corinthians 4:1-4 "Therefore, since through God's mercy we have this ministry, we do not lose heart. Rather, we have renounced secret and shameful ways; we do not use deception, nor do we distort the word of God. On the contrary, by setting forth the truth plainly we commend ourselves to every man's conscience in the sight of God. And even if our gospel is veiled, it is veiled to those who are perishing. The god of this age has blinded the minds of unbelievers, so that they cannot see the light of the gospel of the glory of Christ, who is the image of God.

Billy didn't see God because he was an unbeliever. The word tells us not to use deception or distort the word of God, but to speak truth to every man. That is what I did every day...I spoke to Billy lovingly and shared with him my prayers for him. He knew I loved him and he knew that I believed God loved him even more. He really didn't know what to do with that information. He cursed at me...he rolled his eyes...he didn't want to hear the truth. However, I believed within my heart that Billy was sent there to hear the truth.

I continued over several months to teach Billy the Word of God. I took every opportunity during the daily English lesson to incorporate the goodness of God. Billy was not a bad student, he made decent grades and his behavior was fine, aside from his attitude when God was mentioned. I overlooked it because I knew the source of his anger. Satan was attacking his mind, while God was drawing his spirit.

To make a very long story short, the day came when Billy was leaving the school to move to a different town. I was in the middle of class when a knock at my door made me turn my attention to the Principal that was standing there. He asked the students to excuse me, as I was needed in the hallway.

I excused myself and exited the room. Billy was standing outside my door. I was surprised to see him, but not so surprised at the reason. He spoke to me in a calm tone while saying his goodbyes to me. He said he just wanted to see me before he left because I was his favorite teacher. My heart sank, but my spirits rejoiced at his words. I commenced to tell him how I wished for his future to be prosperous. He reached out to shake my hand and paused. I waited a few seconds as he held my hand. He then spoke, "Mrs. Hart, would you please pray with me before I leave?" Needless to say, the spirit inside me jumped. Joy flooded my face as tears began to flow down my cheeks. I prayed a prayer of thankfulness for Billy and then, before I went on, he spoke again. He told me he was ready to accept the God that I served. He said he knew I was right about it all and that he was ashamed of the awful things he used to say against Jesus. I led him to the Lord that day and have never forgotten his face as he asked Jesus into his heart. His eyes were so different. I said goodbye to him knowing that he would be just fine. However before he left I made sure to tell him of the great battle that he would face in life. He thanked me and said he would stand guard with his armor on; this is one thing I pressed strongly each day...to keep your eyes on the prize and never lay down your armor. I couldn't believe he retained so much of my words.

I share the above story frequently with others to encourage them to never give up on people. There is always hope. God loves us and wishes no one to perish. With that truth I have peace.

Remember, if you feel like you are talking to a brick wall...you probably are, however every wall can be knocked down. That is what happened with Billy...his walls came tumbling down...Hallelujah. I think of him often and I pray that wherever he is, he is still serving God. I pray he has become a mighty man and bringing others to Christ as well.

THINK ON THIS...

What does it mean to you to witness to others?

When you come across that "brick wall" when witnessing, what is your next course of action?

NOTES

QUOTE

"It is Satan's constant effort to misrepresent the character of God, the nature of sin, and the real issues at stake in the great controversy. His sophistry lessens the obligation of the divine law and gives men license to sin. At the same time he causes them to cherish false conceptions of God so that they regard Him with fear and hate rather than with love.

The cruelty inherent in his own character is attributed to the Creator; it is embodied in systems of religion and expressed in modes of worship."

— *Ellen G. White, Great Controversy: Between Christ and Satan*

Chapter

4

BE STEADFAST

I don't know of many people who like someone who is non-consistent...wishy-washy...up and down in their personality or decision making. So, why do we do it in our Christian walk? I am serious. Why do we go up and down in our church going...our giving...even our Christian disposition? We are here to be used as vessels of God...a tunnel for His light to shine through...a voice for Him to speak directly to people. Why do we take that position in Him so lightly. We shouldn't. It should be our number one priority in life; to serve Him by serving others. The enemy loves to toy around with us on this one, doesn't he?

WE NEED TO REMAIN STEADFAST

Not wavering in our choices or beliefs...

Our actions...

Or our compassions.

Be consistent in your walk with God. When you lose consistency, you take off a piece of your armor, therefore leaving yourself vulnerable to an attack of Satan.

Proverbs 9:10 says,

"The fear of the Lord is the beginning of wisdom, and knowledge of the Holy One is

understanding. For through me y
many, and years will be added to you

C.S. Hart

ro

To have Spiritual wisdom, is to purge yourself of traits which are detrimental to you.

Examples:

- **Unforgiving attitudes**

- **Jealousy**

- **Laziness**

- **Excuses**

- **Disobedience**

Don't fall into the trap of undesirable personality traits. Do you see any of the above traits in the mirror in the morning when you do your wake up ine? To say goodbye to the undesirable attitudes in your life, you need to focus more on the purity of God. Remember...the longer you search the deeper you become, and the deeper you go with God the more PURE you become. That is your desire, isn't it? It is mine. I want a desirable personality. I want to be a pleasant person to be around.

We all sin and fall short of the Glory of God, however, our goal should be to daily strive for righteousness.

Remember, God is with us even before we acknowledge He is. In other words...He is waiting patiently for us to realize our need for Him. Realizing this caused me to love Him even more. For God to love me enough that He waited until I cleared my eyes of the mud and muck of this world, and then lovingly took me into His arms, was such a beautiful and undeserving thing. I am so thankful for His patience. Did I deserve it? Of course not. Nothing I could ever do would deserve such love, however He loved me. How amazing it that? AMAZING I say.

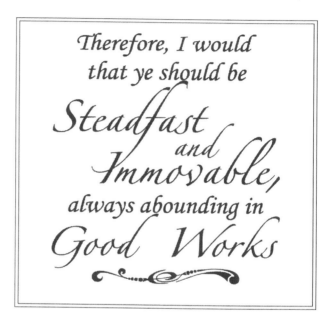

Therefore, I would that ye should be **Steadfast** *and* **Immovable,** *always abounding in* **Good Works**

Something I want you to always remember is this: When we are weak with our armor off...He can carry us...however, we cannot experience VICTORY until we pick it back up. **(Does that make sense?)** I sure hope you understand this. He is there, always;

but our Victory comes in our STRENGTH....our deliberate CHOICE to be an armor bearer.

The next issue I want to talk about is pride. That five letter word...**P R I D E** !

Pride can create deception. Satan loves to use this little five letter word to cause a whole heap of trouble. Pride can lure Christians into a big, deep, dark crevice which can be very difficult to climb out. I have seen it happen in so many people's lives. Why do we let it happen?   Because pride is very sneaky...you can be in the pit before you even know it.

PRIDE AT HOME

Marriage is a big example. My husband and I have found this to be a problem so many times. There are not many people I have ever run across, that will admit they like to be wrong. Most people don't want to be wrong and hate to admit it when they are. When they feel challenged, they immediately go into defensive mode, and before they know it...they are in a full-fledged marital fight.

The right one doesn't like being called wrong....the one in the wrong doesn't like be called on it...therefore, causing a big, giant mess that is likely to take much longer to clean up than it was to make... (whew...what a mouthful of problems)!!!

If you are married, read the following quote *and never forget it...*

"You live in a world at war. Spiritual attack must be a category you think in or you will misunderstand more than half of what happens in your marriage."
— <u>John Eldredge</u>, <u>*Love and War: Finding the Marriage You've Dreamed Of.*</u>

PRIDE AT CHURCH?

Pride can flare up at home...at work...at school...and YES...at church.

Church?

Yes, church...and that is when the enemy starts dancing...happy to see his tactics going to good use.

I have seen so many splits in churches, friendship, marriages and even leadership failings, because of pride. Please don't fall to this snare of Satan. We should always look at church as one thing.

OUR PLACE OF WORSHIP....period.

The word says to forsake not the assembling one with another. God wants us to be there for one another and lean on each other for strength...not to rip each other to shreds when we see failure. Do yourself a favor.....

<u>Rise above Satan's plan.</u>

Be the one who picks the fallen brother up and helps him to his feet, instead of immediately calling up a neighbor and quickly sharing his problem.

If we don't....who will?

It sure won't be the world. The world waits expectantly to see Christian's mistakes....they thrive on it, waiting to say.... "Look at him...he is a so called Christian....such a hypocrite."

Be very careful in your responses to fellow Christians. They need compassion...just as you would if you were struggling....am I right? Yes, you would be desperate for it. I would.

Remain steadfast.

Remain strong in the Lord.

Remain compassionate and loving.

THINK ON THIS...

How does being steadfast and prideful affect each other? Can you be both?

NOTES

Chapter

5

AM I BAD?

The enemy wants nothing more than to make you feel terrible about yourself. His goal is to make you feel unworthy, unloved and unmerited.

Before I go on, read the following;

Names for the Enemy

1. **Abaddon** = (Hebrew : Destroyer) = Revelation 9:11

2. **Accuser of the brethren** = Revelation 12:10

3. **Adversary** = (one who stands against) I Peter 5:8

4. **Angel of the bottomless pit** = Revelation 9:11

5. **Antichrist** = (the one against Christ) I John 4:3

6. **Apollyon** = (Greek: Destroyer) = Revelation 9:11

7. **Beelzebul** = (god of the flies, dung god) Matthew 12:24, Mark 3:22, Luke 11:15

8. **Belial** = II Corinthians 6:15

9. **Devil** = (false accuser, devil, slanderer) Matthew 4:1, Luke 4:2, 6, Revelation 20:2

10. **Enemy** = Matthew 13:39

11. **Evil spirit** = I Samuel 16:14

12. **Father of all liars** (a liar) = John 8:44

13. **God (god) of this world** = II Corinthians 4:4

14. **Great red dragon** = Revelation 12:3

15. **Lucifer** = (Roman rendering of morning star) = Isaiah 14:12

16. **Man of sin** = II Thessalonians 2:3

17. **Murderer** = John 8:44

18. **Old serpent** = Revelation, 12:9, Revelation 20:2

19. **Power of darkness** = Colossians 1:13

20. **Prince of this world** = John 12:31, John 14:30, John 16:11

21. **Prince of the power of the air** = Ephesians 2:2

22. **Ruler of darkness** = (understood as) = Ephesians 6:12

23. **Satan** = (Hebrew = adversary, Greek = accuser) I Chronicles 21: 1, Job 1:6, John 13:27, Acts 5:3, Acts 26:18, Romans 16:20

24. **Serpent** = Genesis 3:4, 14, II Corinthians 11:3

25. **Son of perdition** = (destruction, ruin, waste, loss) = John 17:12

26. **Tempter** = Matthew 4:3, I Thessalonians 3:5

27. **Thief** = John 10:10

Look at all the titles this enemy of ours has been given. Look at number two on the list. Revelation 2:10 says he is the *accuser of the brethren.* He wants us to be put on trial and lose; slander our names and put us to death.

When you feel down on yourself and discouraged, it gives the enemy the fuel to continue burning your self-esteem to the ground. He loves it...he thrives on it...he revels in your destruction. I don't know about you, but I am not willing to allow him any leeway in my life...at least not consciously.

Many people have listened to his lies so much they have started to believe them as well. Are you one of them?

- Do you feel unworthy to be a child of God?
- Do you feel you have secrets that would turn everyone you know against you?
- Are there places you've been that you're ashamed of? Places you would never tell anyone for fear of rejection?
- Things you have thought privately that you feel will keep you from the Kingdom of God?

I have dealt with many of these lies, as I am sure you have. I have come to terms with, and accepted my salvation in the Lord Jesus Christ. I know that through Him I am made a new creature...I have been forgiven and have a heavenly home awaiting me.

Satan can no longer lie to me.

I will not and do not believe his lies.

He continues his tactics, and I know he will until this battle is over.

However, I am made a victor.

God is my Master and I his servant.

Where he leads me I will follow!

When you begin to use the tools that God has laid out before you, you realize that you have the advantage, the upper hand, the power over any situation.

You may say, "whoa, we don't have the power over anything." I will completely agree with you on that. However, when you realize that the Holy Spirit which lives inside of you has ALL the POWER over the enemy, you can be rest assured you CAN overcome.

That makes me excited....!!!! How about you?

The enemy has many titles, many names and many characteristics....don't fall to his demands. Put him and each of his alias's under your feet. Go to the enemy's camp and take back what he's stole from you. AMEN.

The following is an account of an incident which occurred while vacationing with our two children when they were young.

It was a warm day toward the end of summer. My husband's family had rented a strip of cabins on Lake Norfork in a beautiful part of the Ozark Mountains in Arkansas.

We had been looking forward to getting away from the grind of the work week and enjoy some summer sun, swimming and cookouts.

We arrived in the evening, close to sunset and checked into our reserved cabin. It was rustic and homey and we settled right in. There was only one bed in the room, so the kids both slept on the floor in the sleeping bags.

We were tired from the drive and didn't' have to be persuaded to hit the hay early. We were ready to wake up and head out to the water.

Dale had drifted off, as did the kids, (which was a miracle) and I lay there wide awake as usual, due to my chronic insomnia. I remember furrowing my brow in question of the large black shadow on the upper part of the left wall of the room. I was not fearful at this point, just a bit curious.

I recall looking around trying to figure out what object might be creating such a shadow. I turned my head scanning for the source of light, which was needed to implement such a thing.

Nothing...

Just a few seconds had passed when I remember seeing the shadow move.

Yes, move!

Now, I know what you are thinking, but no, I wasn't asleep....or in that have asleep, half-awake twilight state....I was WIDE awake and I knew it.

At this point my mind started spinning. I could feel fear begin to rise up into my chest; that sick feeling you get when you're seriously threatened by something...

or ...someone!

<u>The feeling of being a tiny prey</u>

<u>with a very big predator.</u>

The shadow stretched out and began to move across the wall. It moved over the wall at the end of the bed, and proceeded around to the right side wall as well. I remember it happening as if in slow-motion. I was frozen. I was speechless....literally I couldn't speak! Like my tongue was tethered by an invisible hold.

My heart was pounding out of my chest as the shadow didn't hesitate lifting itself away from the wall. It hovered a second or two before settling down on top of me.

Crushing me...

Suffocating me...

I couldn't scream or even breathe for that matter.

What happened next I will never forget; a lesson in spiritual warfare so real and so important that I use it now much more quickly than I did that night.

I learned my lesson.

As I felt the air being pushed out of my lungs, I realized in my spirit I was encountering an oppression...and evil spirit of oppression; one that wished to see me suffocate right there in the midst of my sleeping family.

I remember realizing in my mind that I had to push the fear aside and cry out to JESUS.

I just recall my mind screaming....

IN THE NAME OF JESUS...

IN THE NAME OF JESUS...

On the fourth round of this desperate request for intervention, I felt the crushing in my chest release as quickly as it captured me. I took a deep breath in, as tears immediately filled my eyes and saturated my face. I didn't hesitate to awaken my husband, who quickly turned the lights and television set on (per my request). He promptly began quoting scriptures to cleanse the room of anything that didn't belong...and a spirit of fear does NOT belong in MY life...

MY FAMILY'S life...

...or YOUR life!

I shared this account with you, not to scare you but to make you aware that the principalities of the world are real....REAL...really real!

You may not ever be directly attacked by one like I did, but they are there...waiting, and if not on guard with your sword and shield at hand, you can find yourself falling for their tactics...which can be very subtle at times.

My cabin experience was very bold and in your face...but I am here to tell you to cry out to Jesus at the slightest threat in your life.

Keep the enemy at bay. You can be rest assured that the name of Jesus will make every entity...

Every demon....

Every devil out there run for cover.

THINK ON THIS...

Think of a time when you really struggled with the enemy; a full on attack...how did you react?

Knowing that Satan is the father of lies...how are you going to react the next time your find yourself under attack?

NOTES

Chapter

6

THE DOUBTING TOOL

Doubt is as important to Satan as a hammer is to a carpenter. It is one of his main tactics to confuse you and discredit God.

He loves for you to question everything and ask...

- Why?
- What?
- Who?
- When?

He wants to confuse you so much about the word of God that you start having disbelief. He wants you to stop using your faith and start using your human reasoning. Reasoning can never **see** who God really is, because reasoning can never **explain** who He is.

- Faith has to be used.

- Faith in His word.

- Faith by knowing that His word is infallible and unchanging.

The first attack against Satan's enemy, (God), was told in Genesis. He came to Eve as a serpent and planned an all-out, cunning, tactical force of attack.

Picture this conversation...

Satan: *Know why you can't touch that tree? Know why you can't have any of that delicious looking fruit? ...That beautiful luscious, juicy fruit?*

Eve: *Why?*

Satan: Because if you take it and eat it, then you will see what He sees. He doesn't want that. He wants to keep you in the dark of all the secrets of this world. He is lying to you. What kind of Master is that?

Put yourself in Eve's place. Would you begin to doubt the goodness of your Maker?

We can't allow ourselves to even begin to doubt a little bit. When we do that, the enemy comes in full force to confuse you even more.

Have you ever had these questions?

- Why do I have to go through this?
- Why can't I pay my bills?
- Why does God allow such pain to be in my life?
- Why do I feel so used and betrayed?

- Why can't I get my way once in a while?

Do any of these questions seem familiar?

The enemy wants you to feel so pitiful for yourself that your faith becomes shattered, broken and wounded. Faith with a crack in it doesn't hold strong in the face of adversity.

Jesus spoke of Satan very clearly in John 8 when he said in verse 44… **"There is no truth in him."**

He warns us very clearly that the enemy is not to be trusted or believed.

Beware my friend…Satan is real and he is mad; and a mad enemy is one to be on guard against. The word says that he is the father of lies. That is a strong title.

It means he is the head over…the master of… and the King of.

He wants you to believe that sin is fun, fantastic and won't harm a hair on your head. He puts things in front of you that seem so harmless at the time, but turn out to be a big fat pit fall; one that causes you to take a head first dive into the muck of destruction.

Let me share with you something I heard a long time ago. I don't remember where or who I heard it from, but it has stuck with me till this very day. It goes something like this...

Satan works in three stages...

First, he wants to keep you from making the decision of salvation. To keep you from thinking you need God in any way. To make you think Christianity is fake, a myth or something losers fall for; those so needy that they have to seek a higher power because they have no faith in their own abilities. However, you have pushed past those feelings and realized your need for Him.

His goodness and mercy.

His mercies which are made new each morning.

Hallelujah you are now a child of God.

An heir to His kingdom.

Second, now Satan has to work harder. He goes to work fast on his next plan of attack. He does everything in his power to work on your mind by discrediting everything you believed in to make you choose God. He wants you to feel stupid, like the decision you felt was so important, now seems foolish. He wants you to be ashamed of it in front of others. He would love nothing more than for you to think you made a huge mistake. He does this in several different ways.

He attacks you right away so you feel like God doesn't really care about you. Your prayers never seem to be answered. You begin to question how real God really is.

All of these things have happened to every believer since the beginning of time. However, it is our decision to continue on and turn away from Satan's lies. When we realize the enemy is having a carnival ride with our thoughts, we can yell down to the attendant,(the Holy Spirit) and say, "*help me, I need You to be with me and clear my mind of these unholy thoughts".* When you make the conscious decision to put the enemy and his tactics under your feet, then you can take that next step up the ladder toward *victory*.

Next comes Satan's **third** tactic; his last but not least trick up his sleeve.

He has put all his efforts into the last two... to no avail.

Now he only has one left.

He realizes that you are never leaving the God that saved you. He knows you have crossed the threshold of victory in your own life. The battle for your soul has just become almost impossible for him at this point. So, he changes his plan. His plan now is the keep you from enlarging the Kingdom of his enemy, God, by keeping you self-focused.

If he can keep you so wound up with your own issues... your own problems...your own situations of trouble... then he knows you will not be in any shape to minister to, or help anyone else.

Your life is the most important and you have to make sure you are happy, right?

Wrong.

When you feel this taking place in your life, think about why you are feeling this way. If you start realizing that Satan is keeping you preoccupied with you own needs, so you never reach out to anyone else, then you can wake up,

and see the light...

smell the coffee...

and win this battle as well!

We were placed here to witness and be spreading the Word of God unto all men.

We have to stay focused, well-fed *(knowledge of the Word)*, and keep our eyed stayed on our calling. What good is a hammer if it's never is used for its purpose. Oh, it will always be a hammer, it will continue to have potential to create something great, but if it never connects with what it was created for, you will never see anything new come from it.

- We have been commissioned to go and witness.

- We have been commanded to preach the good news.

- He uses us as vessels to bring those lost sheep into the flock.

So see, Satan's ***third tactic*** is to keep you from finding any other lost souls, and guiding them in such a path that the Holy Spirit can draw them unto Him.

I try to stay focused on my goal.

My goal is to run this race with such fervor...such diligence, that others want to run with me; leaving my mind open to other's problems and pushing my selfish desires away.

DON'T FALL TO HIS TACTICS...

BE BIGGER THAN THE ENEMY IS...

THE SPIRIT INSIDE YOU SAYS....

YOU ARE GREAT!

THINK ON THIS...

Of the three tactics of the enemy covered in this chapter, which do you feel you are facing right now?

What is your course of action against this type of attack?

NOTES

Chapter

7

BITTERNESS

Don't let hurt feelings or anger cause you to miss out on the blessings of God.

"Don't let the sun go down while you are angry, and don't give the devil a foothold" (Ephesians 4:27).

When another Christian hurts your feelings and wounds you emotionally, you need to address the situation quickly. The longer you let it go, the bigger the animosity grows and becomes detrimental to your soul.

When I say to address the situation, I don't necessarily mean verbally speak out to the person, however, sometimes it has to be done. But overall, you should assess the situation before speaking out at all. Check to see if the person did it on purpose or could it possibly be a personality flaw?

Some people just tend to rub others the wrong way. In this case you should pray for clarity as to what to do. My experience has been to continue loving them and treating them as you would want them to treat you... (Does that sound familiar)?

FORGIVENESS is not something we do for OTHER PEOPLE. We do it for OURSELVES -to GET WELL and MOVE ON.

Yes, it really does pay to turn the other cheek. I am not saying to be a punching bag emotionally for others, or allow anyone to degrade you; but, I do wish for you to pick your battles. Most of the time maintaining you Christian attitude of love and joy through adversary, causes the aggravator to change their advances toward you.

If you do speak to the person, which in many cases is fitting, then do it lovingly with a concern for your friendship and brotherhood. In most cases a bond can grow stronger than even before between the two of you. Not always, but frequently.

Let me share another incident with you from my life. When I was in my mid-twenties I worked for a health facility for the elderly. I quickly made friends with most of the staff and got along well with people...well, most people anyway.

It is hard for me to know that someone may not like me; my personality or attitude, because I always try to be friendly and likable. Not long after I began working there, it became aware to most that I was a devout Christian and loved the Lord with all my heart. I prayed over my meals and shared my testimony with several co-workers. However, there was one lady who I knew, right from the beginning, didn't like me. It didn't take long before she began making comments as I would walk by saying things like,

"Bible thumper",

"She's a Jesus freak",

Or...I love this one..."Religious fanatic".

Needless to say, I had a hard time going to work some days.

I didn't want any persecution.

I have grown to realize that opposition means you are a threat to Satan. Isn't that what we want to be? Yes, I think so.

I dealt with this situation for the better part of a year, and then moved on to a different job placement. It always bothered me that this woman was so adamant about bullying me for being a Christian; however I tried to count it all joy.

Now is the part I have been waiting to tell you... my husband and I visited a new church one Sunday about a year later. We sat about three quarters of the way back in the pews. The service started and the music began to play. The congregation all stood as we began to sing praises to God. I remember the lady in front of me just singing her heart out, lifting her hands toward heaven and worshiping with all of her heart. At the end of the praise time, the minister asked for everyone to meet and greet each other. As the musicians began to play again, the congregation started to mingle amongst each other shaking hands and hugging. The passionate young woman in front of me turned to greet me, and......low and behold....(I am sure I don't have to tell you who it was!) Yes, it was the same lady who gave me such grief for being a born-again, blood-bought Christian.

The blood seemed to drain from her face as she recognized who I was. I am sure the memory of her taunts against me came flooding back to her.

I, as the seasoned Christian, knew exactly what to do and say. Sure, my pride wanted to give her a piece of my mind, however, my Spirit knew better. Instead, I reached out to hug her and commenced to tell her how nice it was to see her in this setting. I praised God for her salvation and focused on her new life instead of her past iniquities. She saw the love in my actions and never spoke a word of the past. We quickly became great friends, and although she never said a word about those early days of our work time together, I knew her remorse. I realized she was young in the Lord, and I chose to move past my feelings and enjoy the future with a new sister in Christ.

PRAISE GOD, she was one more in the Kingdom of Heaven!!!

Think on This

Have you harbored any bitterness toward anyone that you need to let go of?

How has forgiveness affected your life? Forgave someone or been forgiven?

Give an example of forgiveness in the Bible.

NOTES

Chapter
8

WILL YOU WIN?

(Of course!)

Don't ever think that because you have an enemy who wants to see you perish, that you have to succumb to his wishes.   God's word tells us the opposite.   Don't try to use your own tactics and tricks, because believe me we are not a match for Satan....however the *Spirit* inside of us *IS!*

In fact, not only is JESUS a match for the enemy...HE is the demise of the enemy.

What does the Bible say about our enemy?

It names him "Satan"

- ...the adversary
- ...the devil
- ...the dragon
- ...the serpent
- ...the liar
- ...the murderer
- ...the accuser of the brethren

He is evil, hateful, disgusting....do I have to go on again? I know I covered this already, but I want you to be fully conscious of his personalities...and they are multiple.

In *Luke 22:31* Jesus tells Peter, "Satan wants to have you, to sift you like wheat, but I have prayed for you that your faith fail not".

Please be on guard....know that Satan is our adversary...he is clever, vicious and trying with all his might to destroy us.

John knew the key to winning the battle against the enemy. Jesus had a personal conversation with him, and stressed the issue that the BLOOD of the LAMB and dedication to God is the key!

Rev. 12: 11 says,   "And they overcame him because of the blood of the Lamb and because of the word of their testimony, and they did not love their life even when faced with death."

THE BLOOD... How does it work?

First, you need to understand one thing...and when you really get it, I mean **really get it**, you will never be the same.

I promise!

The very moment Jesus sacrificed himself on the cross, is the moment He broke the bondage Satan had on man. The word says that Jesus freed us from our sins by His blood...***HIS BLOOD***! Revelation 1: 5...read it!

Hallelujah! Now that is something to be excited about...*but to be excited you have to <u>get it</u>.*

Deep down in your soul...get it into your heart, mind and spirit...know it, believe it, thrive on it, and pass the word on!

If you don't get it yet, then here is a bit more...

Also, 1 Peter 1:19 says,

"It is Christ's blood that redeemed us."

And....Ephesians 1:17 says, ***"By His own blood He obtained eternal redemption for us."***

Now...if Jesus walked as a flesh and blood man...suffered and was wounded as a human man...bled and died for us as a mortal...then shouldn't we try to understand WHY? I mean seriously....WHY? We all go to church and hear the account of what He did...but do we really get it?

We need to. We desperately need to.

It is the key to overcoming the enemy...for when we realize the immensity of this unselfish gift, is when we gain the power to use it.

If you don't get anything from this book but this one thing, please understand this.....

HE DIDN'T SHED HIS BLOOD FOR YOU, JUST FOR YOU TO LEAVE THE POWER OF HIS BLOOD RESTING DORMANT BESIDE YOU ON THE FLOOR.

PICK IT UP!!!

PICK IT UP...

And the next time the enemy knocks at your door, say, "In the name of Jesus, and by HIS BLOOD, you have to flee." Yes...Speak in your outside voice...yell, scream...whatever it is you have to do to get Satan to understand that you have finally **GOT IT**....

GREATER IS HE WITHIN YOU...

THAN HE THAT IS IN THE WORLD!!!!

Shout it out! Tell the world your testimony. This is how we identify who we are to the world. We are no longer our own, but *His* to do what *H*e will.... **HE PAID FOR YOU**...didn't He? He bought you with a huge price. The least we can do is acknowledge His ownership.

YOU ARE BOUGHT AND PAID FOR!

Shouldn't that call for a big *raise the roof* moment? A shout out at the top of our lungs? A public declaration of our identity with our Savior?

Do not be ashamed of the Gospel of Jesus Christ. Satan wants nothing more than for us to keep our mouths shut.

Be bold.

Be loud.

Be proud!

We are made stronger by our bond with the Lord. Our admission and testimony of His grace will put up a problem for the enemy. He hates bold Christians. He likes weak, insecure and quiet Christians. Do yourself another favor....

BE STRONG IN THE LORD...and acknowledge ALL His good works.

Satan wishes for you to be fruitless.

INSTEAD.....get out there and grow a fruit tree...overflowing with large, juicy and seed bearing fruit.

Jesus defeated the enemy who tempted Him in the wilderness...He did it by using the Scriptures and speaking directly to him. We can do the same. We can and we should. It works.

Be protected. Don't use your own approach to self-protection, but instead, as Paul says, put on the full armor of God. God has a way of protecting every part of you if you put it on. What exactly is it that we're supposed to put on? Truth; righteousness; readiness to share the Gospel; faith; salvation; the word of God; prayer. Do we really trust God's armor? Or are we going to respond in our own way that we think is better?

Don't ignore the reality of spiritual warfare, but instead, as Paul says, be alert. Always keep on praying. If you think it might be spiritual warfare, you should pray. If you are highly confident it is not spiritual warfare, you should still pray. You and I need to develop a life where intercession for others becomes a natural part of our lives.

This book is about acknowledging that you have an enemy, and using the tools God has empowered you with. However, I don't want you to focus too much of your day on the enemy. Recognizing his tactics and giving him attention is two different things.

Recognize...

Regroup...

And Release...

What I mean is this... **Recognize** the enemy and his attack....**Regroup** and get a game plan....then **Release** the Holy Spirit and His protective force over you.

How to do this?.....PRAYER, prayer, prayer!

I love the way Paul puts it. He said, "Pray also for me that whenever I open my mouth, words may be given me so that I will fearlessly make known the mystery of the Gospel for which I am an ambassador in chains. Pray that I may declare it fearlessly as I should." Paul is writing this letter from jail. People want him dead because he is the leader of this crazy, insane religious sect (That really was what they were thinking).

Satan wanted Paul to be afraid, to shut up and stop his mission and calling on his life to preach the Gospel. He wanted Paul to disobey God and give up. So then Paul asks, "Will you please pray that what God has called me to do, I would do it without fear?"

When you become so full of God, you WILL become fearless. You will go through your life doing what He has called you to do.

Don't let Satan think he is winning by having fear. Stand up for Christ. Be bold. Be strong. Be wise. Be VICTORIOUS! You were chosen for this fight and you were destined to WIN!

The Bible says the God of peace will crush Satan under your feet (Romans 16:20), Hallelujah! Also, God has prepared an everlasting fire for him and his demons (Matthew 25:41).

Remember this...Whatever calling you have, whatever you are doing for the Kingdom of God, go and do it know you are guarded by the ONE who *is* the SWORD, the SHEILD and all the armor you need.

HE IS YOUR ARMOR.....HE IS GOD!

THINK ON THIS...

Do you feel like you are winning?

If not, what is it you need?

What makes us more than conquerors?

NOTES

Chapter

9

HOW TO OVERCOME

Yes we are Christians...yes we are saved...and yes we are blood bought children of God, which means we will have a perfect, carefree, pain-free, easy-going, stress-free life, right?

Uh...NOT! I don't think so...never has been and never will be.

Some people think that because they are heir to the greatest throne there ever was or ever will be, they will live life like a wealthy prince or princess here on earth. If you went into your new life thinking this, I am sure you had a quick wake up call.

Hello...

It doesn't take us long to figure out that it really does rain on the just as well as the unjust. It doesn't seem fair, but that is the way it is. Christ commanded us to take up our cross and follow Him, and I promise you that nothing you have to bear could ever compare to what He, as our Savior, endured.

Then you have those people, (which could be you) who think that they could never go up against such an enemy; that this world it just too tough to fight it out with such a supernatural foe.

You're only human, right?

God can't expect you to be able to win over a power like that?

Well, the answer to that is...**YES!**

<u>Absolutely.</u> YES again!

He expects us to use the gift that He has given us to make us battle ready. The Holy Spirit is ready and waiting to guide you and lead you through such a war zone.

God knew what we were dealing with; He knew we would be intimidated by the "Oh no's" and the "What are we gonna do's". But let me tell you this.

YOU CAN DO IT...

YOU CAN WIN...

God would never leave us here unprotected, without a way around, through and out of all our *deep valleys*....our *wide troubles*, and our *high mountains* of problems. He will deliver you through even the largest of setbacks. You are not defeated unless you allow yourself to be. Did you get that?

Are you hearing me? You will not be defeated unless you allow yourself to be. (I thought you deserved to hear that twice).

If we do what God told us to do then we will come out on the other side of adversity to the winning side...we will become **VICTORIOUS!**

Am I sounding like a broken record? If so, then I hope you replay my words over and over. Before you get tired of hearing me I have a few more chapters to go, okay?

Hang in there with me...I know you will be blessed.

Are you feeling my passion?

If you could feel the Jesus bumps (as I call them) running up and down my spine right now, you would be passionate as well...passionate about JESUS! I pray you do. Right now, as you read this, I pray you do.

Sooooo, to continue on, if you do what God's word tells you to do, you will win...Read these scriptures from the Holy Word that gives us that hope of His protection over our lives. When you feel lost and find yourself losing that battle over the enemy, come back to this chapter and read...and read....and re-read.

Deuteronomy 33:27 _"The eternal God is thy refuge, and underneath are the everlasting arms: and he shall thrust out the enemy from before thee; and shall say, Destroy them."_

II Samuel 7:22 _"Wherefore thou art great, O LORD God: for there is none like thee, neither is there any God beside thee, according to all that we have heard with our ears."_

I John 3:8 _"He that committeth sin is of the devil; for the devil sinneth from the beginning. For this purpose the Son of God was manifested, that he might destroy the works of the devil."_

97

<u>Luke 1:77-79</u>　*"To give knowledge of salvation unto his people by the remission of their sins,　Through the tender mercy of our God; whereby the dayspring from on high hath visited us,　To give light to them that sit in darkness and in the shadow of death, to guide our feet into the way of peace."　(II Corinthians 4:6)*

THINK ON THIS...

What does being an overcomer mean to you?

Review this chapter and focus on the one scripture which speaks to you most

NOTES

Chapter

10

PUT ON THE FULL ARMOR OF GOD

You cannot fight this battle on your own. There is no way. You do not have the power, fortitude, or perseverance to do so.

Paul says to put on the full armor of God. For God alone has the power to protect you in all circumstances of adversity. He tells us to protect every part of our being...mind, body and soul. To do so we must find out what this means.

It means these vital traits...

- Truth

- Righteousness

- Readiness to spread the Gospel of His Word.

- Faith

- Salvation

- The Word of God

- Prayer

If we trust in His armor which He has ready and waiting for us to put on, we can trust in His promise that they will protect us...always!

Explanation of the Armor of God

1. God is our armor = Divine protection.

"Finally, by brethren, be strong in the Lord, and in the power of His might" (Ephesians 6:10).

Understanding that we get our defensive power by being **in the Lord**, is when we rise above all strongholds.

"If a man abide not in me, he is cast forth as a branch, and is withered; and men gather them, and cast them into the fire, and they are burned. If ye abide in me, and my words abide in you, ye shall ask what ye will and it shall be done unto you"
(John 15:6-7).

He is our strong protection.

II Chronicles 16:9   Yet, LORD my God, give attention to your servant's prayer and his plea for mercy. Hear the cry and the prayer that your servant is praying in your presence.

He encamps about us.

Psalms 34:   The angel of the LORD encamps around those who fear him, and he delivers them.

He is like a hen to her chicks.

Psalm 91:4   He will cover you with his feathers, and under his wings you will find refuge; his faithfulness will be your shield and rampart.

He is like a fortress of high mountains.

Psalm 125:2   As the mountains surround Jerusalem, so the LORD surrounds his people both now and forevermore.

He is like a wall of fire.

Zechariah 2:5   And I myself will be a wall of fire around it,' declares the LORD, 'and I will be its glory within.'

He is our defense.

Psalm 5:11   But let all who take refuge in you be glad; let them ever sing for joy. Spread your protection over them that those who love your name may rejoice in you.

He is our rear guard.

Exodus 14:20 ...coming between the armies of Egypt and Israel. Throughout the night the cloud brought darkness to the one side and light to the other side; So neither went near the other all night long.

He is our fortress.

Psalm 144:2   He is my loving God and my fortress, my stronghold and my deliverer, my shield, in whom I take refuge, who subdues peoples under me.

He is our rock of defense.

Psalm 18:2 The LORD is my rock, my fortress and my deliverer; my God is my rock, in whom I take refuge, my shield and the horn of my salvation, my stronghold.

He is our hiding place.

Psalm 31:20   In the shelter of your presence you hide them from all human intrigues; you keep them safe in your dwelling from accusing tongues.

He is our place of refuge.

Psalm 46:1   God is our refuge and strength, an ever-present help in trouble.

He is our shield.

Psalm 84:11   For the LORD God is a sun and shield; the LORD bestows favor and honor; no good thing does he withhold from those whose walk is blameless.

As you read over those scriptures I pray you felt His presence; His comfort and compassionate nature.

It is amazing how He has offered us a way to be battle ready, on the front lines and a member of His infantry and win every time.

"Put on the whole armor of God that ye may be able to stand against the wiles of the devil. For we wrestle not against flesh and blood, but against principalities, against powers, against the rulers of the darkness of this world, against spiritual wickedness in high places. Wherefore take unto you the whole armor of God, that ye may be able to withstand in the evil day, and having done all, to stand" (Ephesians 6:11-13). (verses 14-18 following).

He protects us in our daily walk by girting up with truth.

His breastplate of righteousness guards our heart.

By shodding our feet with the preparation of the gospel of peace, it gives us protection for our witness.

He creates us a clean path...a clear way to complete our mission.

Awe...the shield of faith...how I love this one! By taking up the shield of faith we are able to quench the fiery darts of the enemy. COMPLETE PROTECTION.

The helmet of salvation is vital. It protects us from evil thoughts and desires which can steal us quickly and cause severe damage to our minds. Pick it up...put it on....wear it with pride!

The B.I.B.L.E. that's the book for me....

Remember this little bible school song? When you stand on the Word of God, you are holding the Sword of the Spirit...a weapon of defense that can cut down the enemy fast. Carry it with you at ALL times.

And don't forget prayer! *"Praying always with all prayer and supplication in Spirit, and watching there unto with all perseverance and supplication for all saints."*

THINK ON THIS...

The next chapter will be focusing more on the armor of God. Before we get into that, think about what the armor means to you. Why do you feel it is so important to God for us to have it?

Read Ephesians 6: 12-13. Why is the armor important?

NOTES

Chapter

11

WEAPONS

"For though we walk in the flesh, we do not war after the flesh: (For the **weapons** *of our warfare are not carnal, but mighty through God to the pulling down of strong holds;)   Casting down imaginations, and every high thing that exalteth itself against the knowledge of God, and bringing into captivity every thought to the obedience of Christ."*

II Corinthians 10:3-5

NOTE: The Bible tells us we have **weapons.** I want to know what they are...**don't you?** The Bible gives a detailed list of His armor:

Ephesians 6:10-18 *"Finally, my brethren, be strong in the Lord, and in the power of his might. Put on the whole armor of God, that ye may be able to stand against the wiles of the devil. For we wrestle not against flesh and blood, but against principalities, against powers, against the rulers of the darkness of this world, against spiritual wickedness in high places. Wherefore take unto you the whole armor of God, that ye may be able to withstand in the evil day, and having done all, to stand. Stand therefore, having your loins girt about with truth, and having on the breastplate of righteousness; And your feet shod with the preparation of the gospel of peace; Above all, taking the shield of faith, wherewith ye shall be able to quench all the fiery darts of the wicked. And take the helmet of salvation, and the sword of the Spirit, which is the word of God: Praying always with all prayer and supplication in the Spirit, and watching thereunto with all perseverance and supplication for all saints."*

LIST OF WEAPONS

- **The Word of God.**

Ephesians 6:17 "And take the helmet of salvation, and the sword of the Spirit, which is the word of God." The Word is listed as the major offensive weapon. Jesus uses the Word as a weapon.

Revelation 19:15 "And out of his mouth goeth a sharp sword, that with it he should smite the nations: and he shall rule them with a rod of iron: and he treadeth the winepress of the fierceness and wrath of Almighty God." Jesus used it against the devil.

Matthew 4:4 "But he answered and said, It is written, Man shall not live by bread alone, but by every word that proceedeth out of the mouth of God."

Matthew 4:7   "Jesus said unto him, It is written again, Thou shalt not tempt the Lord thy God."

Matthew 4:10   "Then saith Jesus unto him, Get thee hence, Satan: for it is written, Thou shalt worship the Lord thy God, and him only shalt thou serve."

Revelation 12:11   "And they overcame him by the blood of the Lamb, and by the word of their testimony; and they loved not their lives unto the death."

WE MUST READ AND STUDY THE WORD OF GOD. IF WE DON'T KNOW THE WORD, WE CAN'T QUOTE IT WHEN WE ARE BEING ATTACKED!

- **Meditation upon God.**

Joshua 1:8 *"This book of the law shall not depart out of thy mouth; but thou shalt meditate therein day and night, that thou mayest observe to do according to all that is written therein: for then thou shalt make thy way prosperous, and then thou shalt have good success."* Meditation gives us time to hear from God and make strategic plans against the enemy.

Psalms 119:98 *"Thou through thy commandments hast made me wiser than mine enemies: for they are ever with me."* We become wiser than the powers of darkness as we meditation on the Word.

Psalms 19:14 *"Let the words of my mouth, and the meditation of my heart, be acceptable in thy sight, O LORD, my strength, and my redeemer."* Please note the use of the word "redeemer".

Isaiah 26:3 *"Thou wilt keep him in perfect peace, whose mind is stayed on thee: because he trusteth in thee."* The mind is where the battle takes place.

- **Revelation knowledge.**

Daniel 11:32 "*And such as do wickedly against the covenant shall he corrupt by flatteries: but the people that do know their God shall be strong, and do exploits.*" First, we must know God.

I Peter 1:13 "*Wherefore gird up the loins of your mind, be sober, and hope to the end for the grace that is to be brought unto you at the revelation of Jesus Christ;*" Second, we must have a revelation of Jesus Christ.

Proverbs 24:5 "*A wise man is strong; yea, a man of knowledge increaseth strength.*"

Hosea 4:6 "*My people are destroyed for lack of knowledge: because thou hast rejected knowledge, I will also reject thee, that thou shalt be no priest to me: seeing thou hast forgotten the law of thy God, I will also forget thy children."* Third, we need a revelation knowledge to stand against the enemy.

- ### *The prayer of faith.*

James 5:15 *"And the prayer of faith shall save the sick, and the Lord shall raise him up; and if he have committed sins, they shall be forgiven him."* We can take back ground the enemy has taken through sin by praying in faith. Hallelujah, this excites me!

Matthew 17:20-21 *"And Jesus said unto them, Because of your unbelief: for verily I say unto you, If ye have faith as a grain of mustard seed, ye shall say unto this mountain, Remove hence to yonder place; and it shall remove; and nothing shall be impossible unto you. Howbeit this kind goeth not out but by prayer and fasting."* We should enter into spiritual warfare only when we have faith. We are to speak against the enemy in faith. Faith is the key!

Matthew 21:21-22 *"Jesus answered and said unto them, Verily I say unto you, If ye have faith, and* doubt not, ye shall not only do this which is done to the fig tree, but also if ye shall say unto this mountain, Be thou removed, and be thou cast into the sea; it shall be done. And all things, whatsoever ye shall ask in prayer, believing, ye shall receive." Speak to those mountains in your life. Speak out strong and confident, knowing the Word of God is truthful and unfailing.

Ephesians 6:16 "Above all, taking the shield of faith, wherewith ye shall be able to quench all the fiery darts of the wicked." Faith is also our shield against the enemy. Put is on...use it daily...learn to walk in it...practice wearing it, and (never leave home without it).

- **Praise**

I have been a worship leader for many years and I can honestly tell you that singing praises is being a front line soldier. A soldier with a big sword and a massive amount of man power....God power! When

I sing with all my heart and soul, the forces of evil are completely running for cover. They hate hearing us lifting up the majesty of God. Now, I am not saying that praise is just singing...it is not. Praise is how we live daily...how we think about Jesus...how we acknowledge Him in all things. But for me, singing is one of my huge weapons...a weapon I thank God for tremendously.

But don't just take my word for it...

Praise is described as an offensive weapon used against the powers of darkness.

Acts 16:25-26 *"And at midnight Paul and Silas prayed, and sang praises unto God: and the prisoners heard them. And suddenly there was a great earthquake, so that the foundations of the prison were shaken: and immediately all the doors were opened, and every one's bands were loosed."* As Paul and Silas praised, the Lord did warfare for them and opened the doors of the prison. WOW! Wouldn't you have loved to been there at that moment?

I have learned, sometimes the hard and frightening way, to not be fearful of the enemy's fiery darts. When you see them for what they are, (an attack God) you can gain strength by saying, "I will not let Satan hurt God by deceiving me and causing me to fail. Jesus loves us, and He hurts when we hurt...He feels what we feel...And He hates Satan for attacking His people. God allows it, however, to help us grow and learn to lean on Him.

My husband and I have been through many trials, many situations of pain and distress, many hurtful pitfalls and we a realized to count them all joy and rise above them. We can either roll around in our sickness, pity and selfish needs, or we can put on our running shoes and army boots and get this trial over with. Hah! That is my choice...how about you?

THIS TOO SHALL PASS....

I always say this phrase to myself and those around me who are going to something seemingly unbearable.

I want you to remember one of the most important and crucial scriptures, which I am sure you have heard over and over....but when you really focus on it, it becomes alive and so real; a scripture that holds the key to VICTORY....

I CAN DO ALL THINGS THROUGH CHRIST THE LORD....!!!!! *Philippians 4:13*

Remember this....dwell on this...make it your daily focus in all you do.

You gain power through your actions...

PRAYING .

Don't forget to pray for others. Unselfishly and deliberate. We know we are not the only ones who are attacked. Every one of our Christian brothers and sisters battle against the enemy as well.

Prayer is a huge one on the list of spiritual warfare tactics.

Use it...

Embrace it...

Allow it to be second nature.

Interceding on the behalf of others should be a common and constant part of our lives. We are not in this fight alone and we should have each other's back. Jesus had ours when He sacrificed His breath on the Cross. Prayer is the least we can do for others.

THINK ON THIS...

Which Spiritual weapon do you feel you need to pick up more often?

Why is it important to pray for others?

NOTES

Chapter

12

PUT FEAR UNDER YOUR FEET

Yes, you have to recognize your enemy, (Satan and his principalities); however you shouldn't stay too focused on him or his legions. He does not deserve our attention. We do have to be aware and on constant guard, however, we should remain stayed on the gifts and grace of God in our daily lives.

Remember Paul? He told the believers in Ephesus to remain focused on prayer.... Continually. He reminds them to pray for him as he goes about his ministry, teaching and preaching the gospel of Jesus. He knows the importance in prayer. He counts on it.

Not to repeat myself but, remember, he is in jail at this time, he is bound and restrained from his mission. What is he to do? He prays over of the letter he is writing, knowing that it will be blessed and reach its destination. He is a believer...no doubt...no questions...

How wonderful would it be to have the faith of Paul...

- CHAINS WOULD BE BROKEN
- DELIVERANCE WOULD HAPPEN
- WE WOULD BE SET FREE

*The good news.....***WE CAN!**

I worry about people who feel like they can't make it another day in this world. I have heard many say, "I just can't take it anymore". I can honestly say I worry about them, because I too have felt this way in the past. Sometimes I wonder, "*what in the world am I doing writing a book on Spiritual warfare? What could I ever say that would be valuable to someone in battle?*" I do question myself sometimes. I have had my moments of breakdowns, manic moments, and fear beyond compare. Even as I write this the thought pops in my head, "*how can you tell anyone how to fight a battle, when you have been in pit so many times.* Well I can tell you how...It is not through me...

It is through Christ alone.

You see, I have picked myself up after many sleepless nights of despair...not even knowing the cause of my anguish...just knowing I was miserable in my own skin...and come to the realization of Who HE IS! My Father, my Savior, my Friend and my Protector.

Who am I to fear anything?

If you find yourself in a place of despair, a place of confusion; know that the enemy is the cause of it all. He wants to keep you there. Don't allow it. Say no to his advances.

"The nature of the enemy's warfare in your life is to cause you to become discouraged and to cast away your confidence. Not that you would necessarily discard your salvation, but you could give up your hope of God's deliverance. The enemy wants to numb you into a coping kind of Christianity that has given up hope of seeing God's resurrection power."

— Bob Sorge, *Glory: When Heaven Invades Earth*

Bob is right...Satan want you to lose your confidence...your hope. How sad that would be.

This spiritual warfare I keep stressing is very real. It is vengeance on Satan's part...a furious anger toward God and all things good. The battle is raging and whether you believe it or not, it is real and happening as you read this.

Everyday...all day...till the end of Satan's time on this planet.

You are in a battlefield my friend. You are on the front lines and God is equipping you; so go ahead, pick your armor up, put your armor on and WEAR IT PROUDLY!

We all see a world at war. From the ancient of times until now, we have seen bloody battles, loss of lives and wounds beyond repair. But what we visibly see is a drop in the bucket of what goes on in the spirit realm. We cannot comprehend the violent war zone that is being played out all around us. When we realize it, and really...I mean really grasp the concept, then we can stand up proudly against the devil and say, "**God's got this**".

The heavenly realm of angels all around is unfathomable, but they are there...fighting and casting off the devils of darkness trying to get at us.

"Put on the whole armour of God, that ye may be able to stand against the wiles of the Devil"

(Ephesians 6:11)

Satan is described as a roaring lion.

Satan knows your weakness. He knows the things that buckle your knees; the things that cause you to tuck your tail under and run.

Don't go out unarmed and alone.

The biggest battle with Satan is within; within your very being, causing you to have doubt and insecurities, causing you to fall. If you fall, then you will be down when your neighbor needs you. Don't get me wrong, we all fall and get down and need help at times. As long as we are human we will fall.

However....

We need to try to maintain an upright position, knowing who we are, and Who we belong to, and never forget that being a warrior is not just about protecting ourselves but protecting others as well.

- Girt up...
- Be on guard...
- Be battle ready...
- ...and DON'T fall to distractions.

The enemy lays traps out there...pit falls to make you injured and weak. When you are weak you can no longer bear the heavy weight of your armor.

Really?

That is what Satan would like us to think, however when I am weak is when I turn to my Father and say, "God, can you please help me bear this". You know what God says when we ask that of Him? He says, "Child, you don't have to bear the weight of it any longer. It is my battle to fight...let me bear your load". And Hallelujah He is faithful.

How do we make it through this life when we are being attacked daily? At every angle? Around every corner? Well...

We fall down...we get up...but every time we get back up, there we are, in plain sight for the enemy to attack again. Let me ask you...have you ever made it through one day without stress and anxiety, just to wake up the next day to a tornado of problems?

Life isn't about walking in a perfect, problem free world. It is about swimming through the *tidal wave of stress* with your head *ABOVE* water!

THINK ON THIS...

I want you to stop right now...take a deep breath, and ask yourself what God means to you. Seriously, think about it...what does it mean to you to have God in your life?

The answer should excite you...comfort you...and give you peace. If you knew God was standing right beside you every time you face an enemy with a big gun, would you be afraid? Of course not. Picture it...God, in all His majesty, standing right beside you with His strong hand of vengeance, ready to take care of any villain who wants to harm you. You would stand there proudly, knowing your "DADDY", was there ready to protect His child. Well guess what?

He is there.

Standing right beside you.

Every moment. Every day.

NOTES

Chapter 13

RELATIONSHIPS

I touched slightly on this issue earlier, however, now I want to focus primarily on relationships.

Have you ever wondered why relationships are so hard to nurture and grow? How even the most *in love* couple has their share of problems? Some of this is natural and is a part of a healthy relationship; however, far too many relationships fall to break-ups or divorce. Marriages fail because it gets too tough to persevere through the stress of living with another person. People tend to have too high of expectations on their spouse.

Have you ever heard these saying? I am sure you have...

"He just doesn't listen"...
"She nags way too much..."
"He isn't romantic enough..."
"She is way too needy..."

Look at that complaints above. *Yes*, couples separate and divorce for these reasons, believe it or not. The enemy loves to break- up marriages. A major way he does it is to keep us focused on *what others should do for us*, and not what **we can do for others.**

The enemy wants us to feel neglected, unwanted and unneeded by our mate. What if we change those complaints to ...

"I need to listen to her more"

"I really should stop nagging him so much".

"What can I do to make her feel special?"

"I appreciate his help, but I am a capable person."

The problem just changed from, "what can I get?" to "what can I give?"

If we thought like this, how many arguments would be avoided? I don't think I have to answer this question. All of us who are married already know the answer. But stubbornness and selfishness tries to win out every time.

Don't sabotage your marriage by being stubborn! Believe you me, Satan does not want marriage to work.

My husband and I went through many years of struggle; struggle with many of the issues above. Then, he came to me with a practical solution which has given us so much peace in our home.   He suggested we read the Word together daily and have devotion time. I cannot stress enough how this has changed our lives. We look forward to this time together; enjoying a cup of coffee and the living, breathing Word of God to discuss. God never fails to bless us. He is faithful!

Go to church!   Together would be nice. Having a pastor and counsel who teach and are concerned for your spiritual growth is vital. You will find that having a church family is most rewarding. They are an extension of your immediate family. Believe me; it is valuable to know that there are those who have your back in this journey...this battlefield... this fight to the end.   Your relationship will thank you both.

And please, know this...

Your spouse cannot fill that empty hole in your heart. That God shaped hole that only He can fill. So many people want their husband or wife to complete them. You have heard it said so many times... "They complete me". Well, I want you to know this...No human being can complete you. Only the love of God in your heart and soul can fill you to completion. Then, and only then, can you fully love another and *be* loved by another.

GOD IS LOVE....and through Him you find the ULTIMATE LOVE! Go and share it with your mate. Trust me...they will thank you!

THINK ON THIS...

When your marriage gets tough...how do you react? Is this reaction biblical?

How can you change your response, to focus on a more spiritual answer to your problem?

NOTES

Chapter 14

TEMPTATION STRATEGY

Satan is very clever. His strategy is to confuse reality, to make evil seem good. The serpent encountered Eve--- she took the fruit and gave some to her husband.

It was a long time before another ONE said... "Take and eat", and he provided His own body and ransom from their sins.

Written by Gladys Hart

Satan started out, and has continued to deceive, by offering things that only lead to death and destruction.

Jesus provided us with the truth that leads to life. He laid down His life and taught us to do the same; putting aside our own desires to adhere to His will for our lives.

John 15:13   *There is no greater love than to lay down one's life for one's friend.*

THREE TACTICS OF SATAN

1. Boldly --- in your face= fear.

2. Subtly---choices you must make= confusion.

3. Secretly--- hidden attacks coming in the name of Christianity= defeat   (these are the most

dangerous because you can find yourself believing in a lie.

How Does The Enemy Attack? What Are His Plans?

Satan's methods of attack are simple, but in order to dodge his land mines we have to be able to discern them and not fall into the snares.

- **Temptation**

Of course we all know that being tempted is not a sin, but the acting upon a temptation is. When you learn to recognize it as being an evil act against you to cause you to fall, you can avoid it all together. That is where you want to get to, right?

- **Oppression**

Oppression is an inward attack on your spirit; an attack that can leave you virtually lifeless. It can make you feel tired, listless with a lack of interest in daily activities.   Oppression is a spirit which causes mental pain and anguish;   a pain that can cause a Christian to back away from others and stop reaching out for help, (this would be a detrimental action;   we have to lean on others).

SATAN'S UNIFORM OF CHOICE

- **Darkness**

Ephesians 6:12

For our struggle is not against flesh and blood, but against the rulers, against the authorities, against the powers of this dark world and against the spiritual forces of evil in the heavenly realms.

- **Deception**

Psalm 10:7   *His mouth is full of lies and threats; trouble and evil are under his tongue*

- **Ignorance**

Hosea 4:6

...my people are destroyed from lack of knowledge. "Because you have rejected knowledge, I also reject you as my priests; because you have ignored the law of your God, I also will ignore your children.

- **Doubt**

Genesis 3:1

Now the serpent was more crafty than any of the wild animals the LORD God had made. He said to the woman, "Did God really say, 'You must not eat from any tree in the garden'?"

Let's not forget other tactics such as **intimidation** and **confusion**. Do not let yourself become intimidated by Satan and his tricks....he is not worth it. Do not fall into confusion....remember Satan is the father of lies...*so nothing he says is true anyway.*

THINK ON THIS...

When you feel an immediate attack from the enemy, what is your response? What is your first course of action?

Give yourself a break...Trust God and His power; relax a bit and don't struggle so much. He can take care of it. Remember that little word...*Faith!*

NOTES

Chapter

15

JUST ME

There was a point in time when I was suffering greatly from manic depression. I thought I was losing my mind and falling into insanity. The fear was real.

The fear was crippling.

The fear was unforgiving.

Being rooted in Christ and the knowledge of His power had taught me to stand strong, and if I did

He would deliver and restore me. My body was worn out from struggling with emotions that were so overwhelming they almost drowned me. My family tried to maintain security for me, (which I give them credit for hanging in there), I realized they suffered right along with me; they were so patient.

It would have been so easy to let the disease win. To stay medicated to the point of numbness. However, I knew that my cross was to deal with the pain, and find a path through and out of the huge valley I was in. God allowed me to be in that valley so I could grow spiritually and learn to lean on Him.

My path was in front of me. Christ walking ahead; me paving my way through the fiery darts of Bi-polarism. He led me out of the pain of suicidal thoughts and hopelessness. The disease is real...as real as cancer. The ups and downs were so draining. I am sharing this intimate part of my life so you can

KNOW without a doubt that deliverance from ANY attack is possible. Satan thinks he can create so much fear in you that you will just throw in the towel. As I type these words to you, I am praying you will understand how serious your persistence in this journey is. Be solid...

Be real with yourself...

Be humble...

And most of all...BE BOLD!

Put that foe where he belongs.

You are probably saved, blood bought and sanctified, but if you are not and you are reading this book, then it is not a coincidence. It is not just an accident these pages have fallen into your hands.

There is a reason...

A BIG reason...a SUPERNATURAL reason.

Is there something you are struggling with right now....right now as you read these words? I am not there with you, but someone is...someone I know very well; the One who has given me peace, grace, mercy and joy through such an inconsistent life.

A life that is unpredictable and disappointing.

A life that can cause pain and suffering.

Disillusionment...

Anger...

Strife...

All the things that can cause doubt in a loving God.

Trust me friend...He loves you and hates the games that Satan plays. God wishes no man to perish; He only wants for you to trust...believe and know that He is there for you through it all.

Pain and suffering is and will always be a cross we have to bear as mortals; however, there is good news!!! We will not always be mortal....

FOR THE MORTAL SHALL PUT ON IMMORTALITY!!!! Hallelujah....

(That calls for two Hallelujahs)

For anyone who knows me, hallelujah is part of my daily vocabulary. Try it...shout it out! It feels good.

I have so enjoyed writing this book...and although it has brought on difficulties in concentration, (I am sure the enemy did not want it completed) I have finished, making my deadline and singing praises in doing so.

NOTES

Chapter

16

IT'S A WRAP

To wrap is all up....it is about GOD....

He is not just a loving Creator, but a vengeful Father, Who is ready to fight for His children.

I suggest for you, as a child of God, to study about your Father, learn His characteristics and choose to walk with Him every moment of every day.

I get so excited when I think of the love He has for me. When I realized this, I immediately wanted to learn everything I could about Him. I would like to encourage you to seek Him out with all your heart.

Scriptures for Meditation

- *"And without faith it is impossible to please Him, for he who comes to God must believe that He is and that He is a rewarder of those who seek Him."*

Hebrews 11:6

- *"Seek the LORD, All you humble of the earth who have carried out His ordinances; Seek righteousness, seek humility.*

Zephaniah 2:3

- *"Seek the LORD and His strength: Seek His face continually.*

     1 Chronicles 16:11

What I want you to get from the entirety of this book is this....

1.   If you are not born again...get that way! It is the most important decision of your life. It really is a matter of **LIFE AND DEATH**!

2.   Study on the armor of God and **PUT IT ON**....wake up with it on and go to sleep with it on. Don't be caught unprotected.

3. Be on the lookout for the enemy's traps...they are everywhere...(some easy to see and others hidden...so beware).

4. Focus on God and His goodness, but don't underestimate the power Satan has over your mind; he is tricky...and he has no place in your life!

5. Look back at your life and learn from your mistakes. Listen to other's testimonies and learn from them as well. (We are here to help each other in this walk.)

6. And absolutely....100% be looking for Jesus...**His return is near** and we need to be found with our armor on, ready and waiting.

SOOOOOOO...

Step up to the front line!
Be ready to fight the good fight!

And get yourself ready for your grand reward!!!

ETERNITY WITH HIM!

I hope this book has put a passion in your heart, a skip in your step and those (ghost bumps) running up and down your spine!!! The enemy can just back off, for we are made more than conquerors.

I leave you with three things from my life to yours...

HE IS OUR HOPE!

HE IS OUR LIFE!

HE IS OUR BREATH!

And that, my dear friends, calls for one last HALLELUJAH!

About the Author

C.S. Hart was born in St. Louis, Missouri, but considers herself a country girl. Her formative years were spent in the small Arkansas town of Pocahontas, where she graduated high school. As a college student she loved creative writing where she excelled in storytelling.

She attended college at Black River Technical College for her associate's degree and continued on to get her Bachelor's degree at Williams Baptist College in Walnut Ridge, Arkansas. She studied English, Literature and History Education and graduated with honors.   She has won several writing awards, including the award for Creative Writing during her college graduation. She is the author of the Christian suspense novel, *WindStone: The Secrets Within*, *On Enemy Lines*, *A Guide to Spiritual Warfare*, and the children's series, the *Piper Chronicles*. She has also written numerous short stories, some of which are published, including *Grandpa Tom* and *The Chair*.

She has always been drawn to suspenseful tales. Her mind tends to drift in the thriller direction. She tells stories which have a good versus evil story line, while supplying twists and turns and suspenseful page turning plots.

Being a devout Christian, she spent several years working as a missionary in various countries; Brazil being one of them.   This is where she was exposed to the voodoo practices.   She made it a mission to learn about their religion, all the while exposing them to Christianity.   The idea for Windstone: The Secrets Within didn't come until years later.

She spends most of her days writing. She has a number of projects in the works, which will be released in 2014. She is a singer songwriter as well, and travels with her husband and their music ministry, HartStrings Ministries. The attend Warrenton Community Church in Warrenton, Missouri.

She has two children, Brittany and Christian and a son-in-law, Andrew. She lives with her husband, Dale, and their two feline babies, Sugar and Spice, on the outskirts of St. Louis.

Also from C.S. Hart

WindStone: The Secrets Within;   A novel of suspense.

Found online at Amazon.com, Barnes and Nobel and Books–A-Million. Kindle version also available.

Willa Montgomery is facing a real enemy; an enemy that wants to see her dead. Will she survive this long journey and find deliverance, or will she succumb to the horrifying reality of insanity?

62412781R00092

Made in the USA
Lexington, KY
06 April 2017